Diplodocus

By Joanne Mattern
Illustrations by Jeffrey Mangiat

Reading Consultant: Susan Nations, M.Ed.,
author/literacy coach/consultant in literacy development
Science Consultant: Darla Zelenitsky, Ph.D.,
Assistant Professor of Dinosaur Paleontology at the University of Calgary, Canada

WEEKLY READER®
PUBLISHING

Please visit our web site at www.garethstevens.com.
For a free color catalog describing our list of high-quality books,
call 1-800-542-2595 (USA) or 1-800-387-3178 (Canada).
Our fax: 1-877-542-2596

Library of Congress Cataloging-in-Publication Data

Mattern, Joanne, 1963–
    Diplodocus / by Joanne Mattern ; illustrations by Jeffrey Mangiat.
       p. cm. — (Let's read about dinosaurs)
    Includes bibliographical references and index.
    ISBN-10: 0-8368-9416-2   ISBN-13: 978-0-8368-9416-5 (lib. bdg.)
    ISBN-10: 0-8368-9420-0   ISBN-13: 978-0-8368-9420-2 (softcover)
    1. Diplodocus—Juvenile literature. I. Mangiat, Jeffrey, ill. II. Title.
QE862.S3M33223   2009
567.913—dc22   2008025002

This edition first published in 2009 by
Weekly Reader® Books
An Imprint of Gareth Stevens Publishing
1 Reader's Digest Road
Pleasantville, NY 10570-7000 USA

Executive Managing Editor: Lisa M. Herrington
Creative Director: Lisa Donovan
Senior Editor: Barbara Bakowski
Art Director: Ken Crossland
Publisher: Keith Garton

Printed in the United States of America

1 2 3 4 5 6 7 8 9 10 09 08

Table of Contents

Boldface words appear in the glossary.

One Long Lizard!

Diplodocus (dih-PLOD-uh-kuss) was one of the longest animals that ever lived. It was longer than two city buses!

This dinosaur had a long neck that helped it reach food. A long tail helped it balance.

neck

tail

7

Diplodocus had big legs
but could not run fast.
It may have used its tail
to fight off **predators**.

9

Finding Food

This **herbivore** (HER-buh-vor) ate only plants. Its favorite food was probably pine trees. The huge dinosaur ate a lot of plants each day.

Diplodocus was too big to walk into a thick forest. Instead, it stuck its long neck between the trees.

Diplodocus had big teeth shaped like pegs. Its teeth were good for pulling leaves off trees.

Herds and Hatching

Diplodocus traveled in a group called a **herd**. These dinosaurs lived 150 million years ago.

herd

17

Diplodocus was a kind of dinosaur called a **sauropod** (SAWR-uh-pahd). Scientists think many sauropods laid eggs in nests.

Scientists have found its **fossils** in western North America. They study the fossils to learn more about Diplodocus.

Wyoming

Utah

Colorado

New
Mexico

UNITED STATES

North

West — East

South

KEY

= Diplodocus lived here

21

Glossary

fossils: bones or remains of animals and plants that lived long ago

herbivore: an animal that eats plants

herd: a large group of animals

predators: animals that hunt and eat other animals

sauropod: a large, plant-eating dinosaur with a small head and a long neck and tail

For More Information

Books

Dinosaurs Big and Small. Let's-Read-and-Find-Out Science (series). Kathleen Weidner Zoehfeld (HarperCollins, 2002)

I Am a Diplodocus. Karen Wallace (Hodder Children's Books, 2005)

Web Sites

Dinosaurs for Kids: Diplodocus

www.kidsdinos.com/dinosaurs-for-children.php?dinosaur=Diplodocus
This site has fun facts, illustrations, a map, and a time line.

Zoom Dinosaurs: Diplodocus

www.enchantedlearning.com/subjects/dinosaurs/dinos/Diplodocus
Find facts, pictures, maps, and printouts of Diplodocus.

Index

About the Author

Joanne Mattern has written more than 250 books for children. She has written about weird animals, sports, world cities, dinosaurs, and many other subjects. Joanne also works in her local library. She lives in New York state with her husband, four children, and assorted pets. She enjoys animals, music, reading, hiking, and visiting schools to talk about her books.